A-Z OF SKYLANDS

PUFFIN

Published by Puffin 2013
A Penguin Company
Penguin Books Ltd, 80 Strand, London, WC2R 0RL, UK
Penguin Group (USA) Inc., 375 Hudson Street, New York 10014, USA
Penguin Books Australia Ltd, 707 Collins Street, Melbourne, Victoria 3008,
Australia (A division of Pearson Australia Group Pty Ltd)
Canada, India, New Zealand, South Africa

Written by Cavan Scott

www.puffinbooks.com

ISBN: 9780141348919
001
Printed in China

ALWAYS LEARNING   **PEARSON**

Contents

Intro

Welcome, young Portal Master. As you know, Skylands is a wondrous (and sometimes wicked) place found at the very heart of the universe.

This book is your ultimate A to Z of the many things you may encounter as you explore this magical realm. On your travels you'll find enchanting locations, loathsome lairs, magical objects and marvellous myths.

And then there are the heroic Skylanders, brave champions who have pledged to protect Skylands from the minions of Kaos and the forces of Darkness.

To help you on your way, Master Eon has provided you with your very own Sidekick guide. You'll find him alongside this very book. He makes for a handy companion and no mistake!

How to use your Skylanders Spyro's Adventure™ Sidekick

Want to add your Sidekick to one of your Skylanders games? Just pop him onto your Portal of Power. In a flash, your tiny chum will burst into life in your game, following your Skylander around on screen.

Aa

Arbo

Born in the ruins of Eon's Citadel, Arbo is the son of Barbo and grandson of Larbo. He is an Ent, a race of green folk who hail from the Tree of Life. Like all Ents, Arbo can communicate with plants, from the oldest tree to the youngest sapling. Happiest when communing with nature, this truly spiritual flower child sees the good in everyone (except for sheep and trolls of course).

Air Element

One of the magical Elements that bind all things together in Skylands.
Air Skylanders can often control the wind or other, weirder weather systems.

Air Spell Punks

These mean mages can create gusty barriers from thin air.

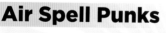

Arkeyans

10,000 years ago, Skylands was ruled by huge robots known as the Arkeyans. These mechanical menaces discovered a way of fusing magic and technology and ruled Skylands with an Iron Fist – literally.

They enslaved Mabu, Molekin and Gillmen alike, forcing them to build brilliant but terrifying weapons.

Finally, the free magicians of Skylands decided enough was enough. They gathered the very first Skylanders – known as the Giants – and sent them into the City of Arkus to fight the Arkeyan King. The technological tyrant was defeated and the Arkeyans themselves fell into eternal sleep.

As the centuries passed, the Arkeyans were forgotten, their terrible technology and vast riches locked away in deep underground cities.

No one knows why the Arkeyans chose to live beneath the ground. Perhaps it was due to their peculiar weakness. While they had no problem remembering things above or to the side of them, they often forgot things below them. This meant that instead of burying treasure they hid their wealth high above their heads. Odd.

Arkeyan Armory

The last resting place of the Arkeyans' deadliest weapons. Convinced that the countless automated defence systems would keep the Skylanders at bay, Kaos hid the Eternal Magic Source within the Main Vault. He was wrong.

Arkeyan Bombers

Watch out. These Arkeyan robots just love chucking balls of crackling energy at their enemies. Fortunately for you, they're not the brainiest of 'bots. Throw their plasmoid balls back and they'll explode in their metal faces.

Arkeyan Crackler

These shifty Arkeyan warriors create a squadron of duplicates to confuse and confound. Destroy a double and the Crackler will just conjure another in its place. You need to pay attention to get the upper hand. Crackler clones move as one.

Spot the one acting independently and you've found the original.

Arkeyan Duelists

Anyone who says the pen is mightier than the sword has never met an Arkeyan Duelist. These dark and stormy knights wield massive blades, and become invincible when they drive their swords into the ground.

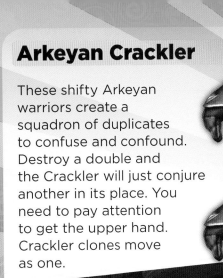

Arkeyan Shield Juggernauts

Not only do these hulking robots carry indestructible shields, they also fire powerful laser beams. Nasty.

Arkeyan Jousters

These mace aces launch shocking attacks with their electrified staffs.

Arkeyan Snipers

Sneaky snipers who hide in holes and wait for unsuspecting victims. Come near and they'll pop up to blast you with deadly rockets. When they're not lurking around Arkeyan cities, the silent assassins enjoy a game of peek-a-boom.

Arkeyan War Machines

The mothers-of-all-mechanoids, Arkeyan War Machines tower over their enemies. In fact, they tower over most of their friends too. Armed with laser-vision, the War Machines are also handy with their fists. They float like mammoth-sized butterflies and sting like humongous bees. Just make sure you're not standing beneath one if they get knocked out. The bigger they are, the harder they fall.

Armored Chompies

Like Chompies, but with added armor.

Auric

Able to sell snow to ice ogres, Auric loved making money from an early age. Rumour has it that his first words were 'balance sheet' and he started selling goods before he could even crawl. These days, the industrious merchant runs a chain of boutiques providing Skylanders with mystical objects, magic potions and super-tough Skystones.

Axe Reaver

The legendary weapon of the Ooga Orcs. Attached to a zip-line, Axe Reaver can be swung in an arc or sent smashing into enemy lines. It's also remarkably good at slicing up vegetables.

Axecutioners

Axecutioners are cyclopses with a difference – they have two eyes! They also have a huge axe to grind. Stand too near and the Axecutioner will take a swing. Move further away and the bi-ocular brute will simply toss its weapon at you. Like a boomerang, an Axecutioner's axe always comes back.

Bb

Bag O' Booms

These lumbering cyclopses lob bombs at anything that moves. The silly nits don't always remember to light the fuses though.

Bambazookers

Solitary forest dwellers who have stood in the same spot for as long as anyone can remember. They even stayed put when Zook decided to go wandering.

17

Bark Demons

A monster with a bite definitely worse than its bark. One minute they look like normal trees and the next they're trying to chew your head off. If you manage to avoid their gnarled old arms, these terrible trunks will send a root snaking towards you. One touch and a full grown tree will erupt from between your toes.

Barkley

Tree Rex's titchy Sidekick. Don't underestimate his size. From tiny acorns, mighty warriors grow.

Bash

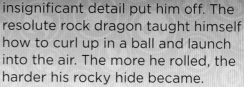

From an early age, Bash wished he could fly. There was only one problem – he was a dragon without wings. Not that Bash let that tiny, insignificant detail put him off. The resolute rock dragon taught himself how to curl up in a ball and launch into the air. The more he rolled, the harder his rocky hide became.

One day, a band of hunters swept into the valley, catching dragons in their airship's net. Alone on the ground, Bash thundered off the side of a cliff. Shooting through the air like a cannonball, he smashed through the ship's hull, freeing the trapped dragons.

Eon was so impressed with Bash's bravery that he made the rock dragon a Skylander before he'd even crashed back to earth. While he's still a little touchy about his lack of wings, one Skylander is always sure to warm his cold stone heart – Bash has a soft spot for the beautiful Flashwing.

Battle Cries

Skylanders shout their battle cries whenever they jump through a Portal of Power. Every year they hold the Annual Battle Cry Contest to see who can yell theirs the loudest. Other rounds include the most frightening battle cry and the battle cry most likely to make milk shoot out of each other's noses.

DROP THE HAMMER!

Battlefield

The Battlefield is a particularly war-torn area of Skylands. The Troll Army often tests its latest weapons here, including the catastrophic Mega Bomb, devastating super tanks and the actually-quite-underwhelming custard grenades. No wonder the Eternal Tech Source was hidden here.

Batterson

When he struggled to sell his pies to his fellow Molekin, Batterson the baker tried to sell pastries to the Undead instead. The pies became so popular that the denizens of the Underworld even stopped eating brains. Now, Batterson sells pies all across Skylands. His best selling line is cheese and sheep wool pasties. Yum!

Benevolent Ancients, the

The mysterious race that built the Core of Light. Unfortunately, the Ancients were as lazy as they were wise and, after creating the Core, they all decided they deserved a nice long nap. When they finally awoke they discovered that 100,000 years had passed – so they went back to sleep again.

Blastaneers

Squid-faced pirates who carry cannons on their shoulders. No one knows where they keep their cannonballs. Best not to ask.

Blaze Brewers

If you can't stand the heat, stay away from the Blaze Brewers and their blistering flamethrowers.

Blade Witches

Evil Drow sorceresses known for throwing large curved blades at people. They also sharpen their ears twice a week and bathe in sour cabbage milk. Ugh!

Blitzer Bullies

Not only do these Goliath Drow carry two spiked shields wherever they go, they also never leave home without strapping Life Spell Punks onto their backs. It's a win-win situation. The Bullies get their injuries healed and the Spell Punks save on shoe leather. Or rather they would, if they only had feet.

Blobbers

A knowledgeable Mabu with little in the way of common sense. Easily hoodwinked, Blobbers was tricked into working at Cutthroat Carnival. Promised as many

churros as he could eat, he didn't check his contract's small print. Not only was he unpaid, but he didn't get a minute's holiday either. And he soon got sick of churros too . . .

BOOM!

1. Flynn's catchphrase – usually used after he's told everyone how great he is. Which happens a lot.
2. A popular game for trolls. No one really understands the rules (if there are any) but it's basically fetch with Chompies and live dynamite. Other troll games include minefield racing, barbed wire tug-of-war, how many explosives can you hide in your pants, and hand grenade juggling.

Boomer

Ever since he was a tiny little troll-ling, Boomer has loved blowing stuff up. In particular, he has a lifelong love for the unmistakable sound of fluffy little sheep being sent sky-high by three sticks of carefully placed dynamite. So it was no surprise to his friends and family when he eventually found himself in the TA (or Troll Army).

At first, Boomer loved the military life, as he found that his superior officers had no problem with him blowing things up. In fact, they positively encouraged it, supplying him with all the dynamite his explosion-loving heart desired. But, after a while, Boomer realized that all the TA really cared about was invading places. Just because Boomer liked big bangs it didn't mean he liked war. He knew for sure that the soldier's life wasn't for him when his squadron blew up a dam to flood a nearby Mabu village. Thinking

on his armored feet, Boomer blasted a flock of sheep into the path of the gushing water. Their wool soaked up the flood and news of this troll-turned-good reached Master Eon. The Portal Master invited him to join the Skylanders, but on one condition: from that day on, he could only use his explosive skills to fight evil. Sheep everywhere baa-ed a sigh of relief.

Bouncer

Long before the rise of the Arkeyan Empire, Bouncer was the greatest All-Star Roboto-Ball player Skylands had ever known. Unfortunately, the killjoy Arkeyans considered spectator sports a waste of time. After all, why watch games when you could be building a seven-storey monument to the glory of the Arkeyan King?

Bone Chompies

Undead Chompy skeletons, all tooth and bone.

Bone 'n' Arrows

If you spot a pile of old discarded bones, tread carefully. It could be a Bone 'n' Arrow waiting to strike. Even though these skeletal archers have no eyes, they never miss.

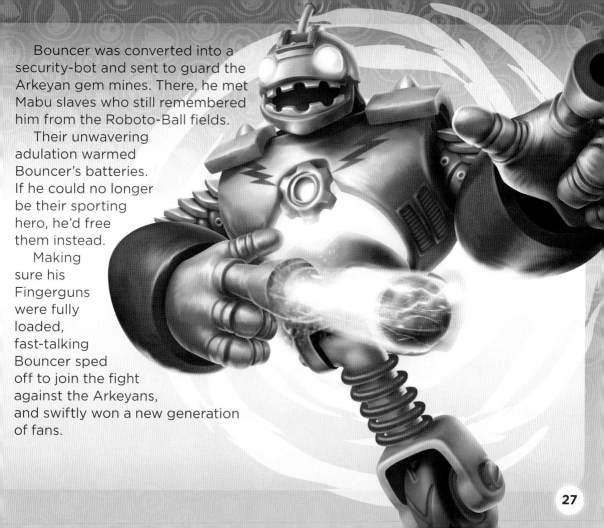

Bouncer was converted into a security-bot and sent to guard the Arkeyan gem mines. There, he met Mabu slaves who still remembered him from the Roboto-Ball fields.

Their unwavering adulation warmed Bouncer's batteries. If he could no longer be their sporting hero, he'd free them instead.

Making sure his Fingerguns were fully loaded, fast-talking Bouncer sped off to join the fight against the Arkeyans, and swiftly won a new generation of fans.

Brock

All Brock wanted to do was keep his Rumbletown neighbours happy. Staging a tournament, the Goliath Drow kidnapped Ermit the Hermit in the hope that a Skylander would come to fight in his arena. It worked – but a little too well. The Skylander defeated Brock's champions and then wiped the floor with Brock as well. Seeing the error of his ways, Brock joined the crew of the Dread-Yacht, organizing arena challenges as part of the Skylanders' training.

Brute

Kaos' prize-fighting scrapper has served the wicked Portal Master for years. In return, Kaos has promised to take the jawbreaker on a fishing trip. But the one thing everyone knows about Kaos is that he never keeps his promises. Poor old Brute.

Cc

Cadaverous Crypt

A doom-laden dungeon full of mazes, shrines and other spooky stuff.

Cali

One of Skylands' most adventurous explorers, Cali thinks nothing of setting out on thrilling expeditions with or without a map. In fact, it was Cali who first discovered many of the weird and wonderful locations Skylands is known and loved for today.

Brimming over with confidence, Cali doesn't let anything stand in her way. She doesn't even mind being captured – which is good, as it tends to happen quite a lot! These days she spends most of her time training the Skylanders and avoiding the attentions of Flynn (although secretly she's quite fond of the old windbag).

Camo

Half-dragon, half-plant, Camo hatched in the roots of the Tree of Life. Bursting with energy, he can make fruit and veg grow at super-fast speeds. There's only one drawback. The magically-grown food explodes before you can eat it – much to mischievous Camo's delight.

Master Eon first met Camo when he spotted a ripe-looking melon on Treetop Terrace. Without warning, the fleshy fruit exploded in Eon's startled face, smothering his beard in pulpy goo. Unable to stop himself from laughing, Camo rolled from his hiding place. Recognizing Camo's potential, Eon asked the dragon to become a Skylander – and to look after his veg patches too.

31

Captain Dreadbeard

One of the scariest and scurviest sky pirates of them all, Dreadbeard has spent many of his days plundering, pillaging and playing pirate cards. However, since he discovered the game of Skystones, he's been a little pre-occupied. While he still loves a good day's pirating, Skystones has become his one true love. He even went as far as to set up Cutthroat Carnival, home of the annual Skystones Championship.

Captain Frightbeard

If you thought Dreadbeard was bad, you'd poop your deck if you ever met Frightbeard. Currently imprisoned within the mystical Chest of Exile for a second time, the snaggle-toothed scoundrel was defeated by the Skylanders when they caught him trying to free his banished crew. Ironically, his own sword now serves as the lock that keeps he and his gang from terrorizing the skies once more.

Chill

Long ago, Chill was the celebrated captain of the Snow Queen's Guard. But Chill became complacent. She ignored warnings of a great cyclops army marching from the South, convinced they posed no threat. But the Snowclopses ice-skated into the castle and captured the Queen from beneath Chill's nose. Driven crazy by guilt, Chill fled from the Kingdom, vowing she would only return once she found the Queen. Now a Skylander, Chill is still searching and, armed with her icy javelin, she always gives evil the cold shoulder.

Chompies

The most common Skylands monster. Chompies are basically mouths on legs – mouths filled with razor-sharp teeth that is. Some scholars, such as Professor P Grungally, insist they only bite you as a sign of affection. Just imagine what they'd do if they didn't like you!

Chompy Bot 9000s

Clod-hopping robots built by trolls and piloted by En Fuego Chompies. Thankfully, because trolls aren't as good at building weapons as they think, the battle-bots often overheat.

Chompy Pits

The Arkeyans often kept their prisoners in underground chasms crammed full of hungry Chompies. Now that's just mean.

Chompy Mage

A powerful, if batty, sorcerer. No one knows why the Chompy Mage loves Chompies so much. Perhaps it's because he likes being chewed. The Chompy Mage dresses like a Chompy, carries a Chompy-shaped staff, owns a Chompy glove puppet and can even transform into a massive slobbering Chompy. His non-Chompy hobbies include karaoke and making enchiladas (which he shares with his Chompies, obviously).

Chompy Pods

Large green plants that spawn a constant stream of Chompies until they are uprooted or destroyed.

Chop Chop

Those Arkeyans just loved to meddle. First they combined magic with technology to create War Machines. Then, they experimented with machines and the Undead to create the Elite Guard. Vast squadrons of these skeletal soldiers swept across the Empire, guarding temples and patrolling vaults. When the Arkeyans vanished, the Guard was left with no one to give them orders. Most fell apart, but one – Chop Chop – picked up his indestructible sword and shield and clambered to the surface to search for a new commander. After 10,000 years of wandering, he met Eon and was enlisted as a Skylander. Now, the powers of Darkness quake at the sound of Chop Chop's bone-chilling voice.

Clam-Tron 4000

The son of General Robot, Clam-Tron 4000 used to transform clams into pearls. However, centuries of rusting on the beach mean the chatty robot can now only produce bombs. Not that he seems to care.

Cloud Kingdom

The home of the heroic Storm Titans.

Conquertron

At the height of the Arkeyan Empire, Conquertron guarded Mabu slave workers. A captive to his programming, he was particularly fond of his 'crush all resistance' and 'obliterate cringing rebels' sequences. After being defeated by a time-travelling Skylander, Conquertron lay dormant until re-activated by Kaos. Impressed by the Portal Master's evil, he joined Kaos in his search for the Iron Fist.

Core of Light

Built by the Benevolent Ancients, the Core of Light holds Darkness at bay. Powered by eight Eternal Sources (one for each Element), the Core was protected by Eon until its destruction at the hands of Kaos. Thankfully it was soon rebuilt, thanks to the Skylanders and a young Portal Master from Earth – you!

Corn Hornets

Nothing ruins a picnic more than having giant stripy wasp monsters attack as you tuck into your jam and pickled meringue sandwich. Unless they sting you as well, which is much, much worse.

Crawling Catacombs

A spider-infested labyrinth of tunnels. Not the best place for flies, arachnophobes or, to be honest, anyone who isn't a spider.

Creepy Citadel

A group of zombies from the Cadaverous Crypt once borrowed the Citadel's skeleton key but forgot to return it. Typical. That's the problem with zombies. They're always losing their memories – as well as various body parts.

Crunchers

The blue-skinned cousins of the Chompies. Once their vice-like jaws have closed, it's a nightmare to shake them off. Ouch!

Crusher

Crusher was only a rock-tot when he first tried on his father's mining helmet. But even then, at the tender age of 3,000, he knew he had to follow in his dad's stomping footsteps. In fact, he knew he had to do better. Crusher Senior was Skylands' best rock pulverizer, so Crusher Junior set out to go one step better. The Earth Giant studied every scrap of rock-lore he could find, and set out on a quest to find Skylands' rarest rocks – and then crush them beneath his hammer.

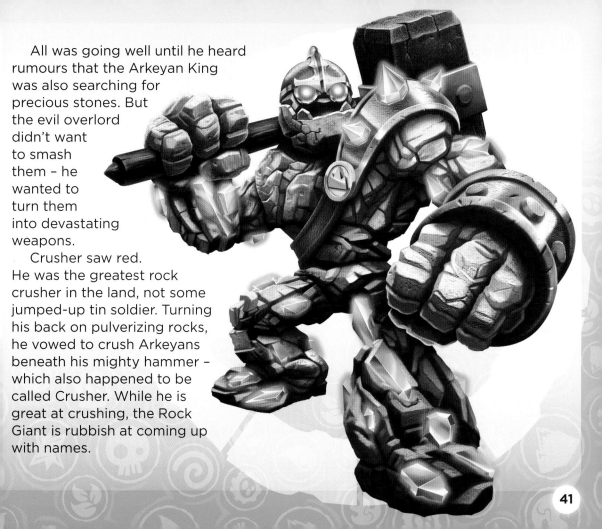

All was going well until he heard rumours that the Arkeyan King was also searching for precious stones. But the evil overlord didn't want to smash them – he wanted to turn them into devastating weapons.

Crusher saw red. He was the greatest rock crusher in the land, not some jumped-up tin soldier. Turning his back on pulverizing rocks, he vowed to crush Arkeyans beneath his mighty hammer – which also happened to be called Crusher. While he is great at crushing, the Rock Giant is rubbish at coming up with names.

Crystal Eye Castle

Named after the Crystal Eye, a vital component of the Core of Light that was discovered by a horde of particularly smelly cyclopses. The Eye was rescued by the Skylanders, but the castle is still there, complete with its all-seeing security eyes and lingering stink.

Crystal Golems

Grizzly, green and generally best avoided, Crystal Golems are protected by a swirling ring of energized gems. To stand a chance of beating these burly bogies, you'll need to smash each crystal before you can get close.

Cutthroat Carnival

Roll up! Roll up! All the fun of the fair! As long as being in mortal danger is your idea of fun, that is. What do you expect from a circus run by a bunch of pirates and buccaneers? That being said, The Oar and Plank does serve a fine pint of sky-goop (whatever that is).

Cyclopses

The stinkiest creatures your nose will ever have the misfortune of smelling. Cyclopses claim that they're allergic to baths, but that's just an excuse. They only remain as pongy as possible because it's the only way the little wimps can be frightening. The sad fact is that your average cyclops is as thick as he is smelly. It's enough to make your eye water.

Cyclops Mammoths

One of the only good things you can say about cyclopses is that they love their pets. Unfortunately, most of their pets are furiously dangerous animals that will bite your head off as soon as look at you. The Cyclops Mammoth is a blue-furred freak that can rip a rock-golem from limb to limb. Luckily, they are mostly kept chained to a post. Unluckily, they're usually strong enough to break free.

Cyclops Navy

Unbelievably, Cyclopses are actually extremely talented stonemasons. Their intricate temples, castles and statues can be found all across Skylands. However, their decision to carve an armada of stone ships didn't go down so well. Actually, thinking about it, that's exactly what it did. The entire navy sank seconds after it was launched. Glug glug glug.

Cynder

Cynder is a Skylander with an extremely shady past. Before she had even hatched from her egg, she was stolen by Malefor, the infamous Undead King of the Dragons. He raised the dragoness as his own, teaching her to strike fear into the hearts of anyone who heard her name. She tore across her homeland, burning down entire villages in her wake.

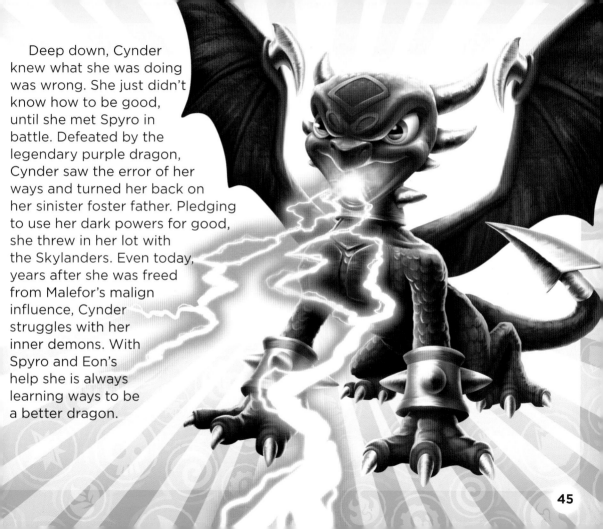

Deep down, Cynder knew what she was doing was wrong. She just didn't know how to be good, until she met Spyro in battle. Defeated by the legendary purple dragon, Cynder saw the error of her ways and turned her back on her sinister foster father. Pledging to use her dark powers for good, she threw in her lot with the Skylanders. Even today, years after she was freed from Malefor's malign influence, Cynder struggles with her inner demons. With Spyro and Eon's help she is always learning ways to be a better dragon.

Dd

D Riveters

Manic trolls armed with rapid-firing plasma rifles. In their spare time, D Riveters collect rare troll mines and enjoy flower arranging. OK, that last bit is a lie.

Darkness, the

The very embodiment of evil. No one knows what the Darkness actually is or where it came from. But everyone knows that it should be feared. Simply put, the Darkness is what monsters have nightmares about.

Dark Spyro

Spyro the Dragon is a unique Skylander. Not only can he harness his natural Magic powers, but he can also manipulate the other seven Elements as well. But this adaptability comes at a terrible price. The purple dragon is susceptible to the dark power of evil magic. This weakness first became known when the Darkness almost overwhelmed the Core of Light. As the skies grew black, Eon was horrified to see a change in Spyro. A wild grin spread across the dragon's usually pleasant face and his scales took on an ebony hue. Before he could be completely turned, Eon cast a protective spell around his trusted Skylander and Spyro returned to normal. Ever since, Eon has trained Spyro to channel sinister magic without letting it consume his soul, fighting Darkness with Darkness itself. It's a risk Spyro only takes in the most extreme circumstances. The danger is that, one day, his darker side will become too strong to resist.

Dark Water Cove

The pirate stronghold where the Core of Light's Twin Spouts of Ocea-Major-Minor were found by the Skylanders. They had been stashed in the Ancient Temple near the top of a waterfall, where the plundering privateers held their pirate auctions.

A
B
C
D
E
F
G
H
I
J
K
L
M
N
O
P
Q
R
S
T
U
V
W
X
Y
Z

Deadly Shark Bath of Dooooomsharks, the

One of Kaos' most deadly spells, not to be confused with the Not-at-all Deadly Puddle of Friendly Tadpoles.

Diggs

One of the Skylanders' closest allies. Even by Molekin standards, Diggs is short-sighted. Amazingly, he still managed to win the annual Speed Tunnelling Championships five years running. The visually-challenged engineer eventually lost the title when, instead of grabbing his trowel, he ploughed into the side of a mountain armed only with an over-ripe banana.

Dino-Rang

Despite his fearsome appearance, Dino-Rang is usually calm and controlled. That is until someone mistakes him for a dragon and feels the wrath of his whirling stone boomerangs. Hailing from a prehistoric plain far, far away, Dino-Rang belonged to a proud tribe of fearsome hunters. No one came close when it came to twirling boomerangs, but his skills couldn't save him when a freak Portal opened beneath his bed one night. The dumbstruck dinosaur awoke to find himself surrounded by a coven of mischievous wizards. He had been transported into a Skylands temple. As the sinister mages closed in, the harassed hunter whipped out his earthen boomerangs and smashed the wizards all the way to the Outlands. Now he just had to get home.

Remembering the legends of his clan, Dino-Rang started searching for the fabled Twin Diamond Boomerangs in the hope that they would transport him back to his tribe. On his travels, the determined dinosaur met Eon, who welcomed him into the Skylanders fold.

Dirt Seas

Until recently, the Dirt Seas were a vast ocean of dunes and dust. Dirt Sharks came from all around to swim through the claggy earth, ride the sand waves or even snorkel beneath the ground. An unexpected explosion, high above the Dirt Seas, put an end to the popular holiday destination. When the blast hit the sand, the ocean was fused into one sheet of glass. Thankfully, Terrafin was on hand to make sure no one was hurt. Phew.

Dolphins

Water Skylander Zap has had a long-running feud with a pack of dolphins. Whenever they race together, the dolphins get their flippers in a flap, claiming that Zap's shocking sea-sludge electrocutes them on purpose. The water dragon denies foul play – he says the dolphins are just bad losers.

Double Trouble

When he was young, Double Trouble didn't have time to make friends. He was too busy learning every spell known to tiki-man. Living alone on a remote tropical island, the spell-caster spent his days foraging for rare flowers and magical roots to enhance his potions and tinctures. But there was one plant he longed to find above all others. The Whispering Water Lily was rumoured to multiply the strength of any spell. So the solitary shaman couldn't believe his eyes when he stumbled upon the legendary flower during a rainforest ramble. Unable to contain himself, he wolfed the flower down and waited for it to take effect.

The first sign that he'd made a mistake was when his stomach started to rumble. Within seconds it had begun to roar. Suddenly, the witch doctor let out a

burp and three tiny copies of himself popped into being. In his eagerness, he had misunderstood the flower's power. It didn't multiply spells – it multiplied the spell-caster. While the diminutive clones were great company (he'd talked to himself for years, after all) there was one slight problem. They exploded on contact! Ooga-booga!

51

Dragons

Many different kinds of dragon roam Skylands. There are water dragons, rock dragons, undead dragons and even a very famous purple dragon. According to the myths of the benevolent Ancients, there was once a race of sheep dragons. This is a thought that plagues Hugo's nightmares.

Dragon's Peak

The home of the Dragon King. In the past, dragons used to vote for their leaders, but no one could understand the polling system. To make matters worse, all the candidates insisted on making long, boring speeches that seem to go on foreeeeeeeeeever. So it was decided that the first one to plonk his backside on the throne would become king. Simple. As it turned out, the fastest dragon, Ramses, was also the wisest. What a stroke of luck.

Dread-Yacht, the

Flynn's faithful airship has a troubled past. Once known as the 'SS Look Out!', the Dread-Yacht was previously owned by a pilot so bad that he decided to invent a machine to make himself more lucky. Unfortunately, he wasn't just a rubbish pilot but also a rubbish inventor, and his Luck-O-Tron device did the opposite of its intended purpose by draining all luck from the cursed craft. He was able to salvage some good fortune however, and tweaked the Luck-O-Tron so that it would help those flying the ship – but only when they're not actually on board. Actually, this could well be why the vessel's previous owner was so keen to sell her to Flynn. Not that the puffed-up pilot believes any of this curse flim-flam. He thinks the old girl is as amazing as he is . . . well, almost.

Drill Sergeant

Like all Arkeyan constructs, Drill Sergeant had been programmed to obey orders come what may. When the Arkeyan empire fell, the powerful bulldozer didn't know what to do, so he stayed put, patiently waiting for commands that never came. As the centuries passed, he was buried deep beneath the ground. His batteries drained and Drill Sergeant shut down, never to wake again.

That is until Terrafin burrowed straight into him on the way back home from a mission. The Dirt Shark pulled the dormant machine to the surface and showed him to Master Eon and the other Skylanders. The Portal Master realized that a spark of life still burned within the tarnished tank and, casting a long-forgotten spell, re-activated the Arkeyan worker. The rust fell from Drill Sergeant's paintwork, his drill-bits began to roll and his eyes blazed bright as they focused on Terrafin. He immediately pledged his allegiance to the Dirt Shark, whose first order was "stop following me!"

Bemused by an Arkeyan-less world, determined Drill Sergeant joined the Skylanders, happy to be useful once again.

pain of being an oversized power-tool. Those who heard his caterwauling are just happy that he's stopped.

Drill-X

Kaos' large, rusty and tone-deaf drilling machine. Drill-X was defeated by the Skylanders after he tried to drill his way down to the Lost City of Arkus. As well as tunnelling into the ground, Drill-X loved to sing. Unfortunately, his voice circuits sounded like two blunt drill-bits grinding together. Some believed that the reason the drill-bot sang was to share the inner

Drill-X's Big Rig

A mobile drilling rig ruled by the tone-deaf Drill-X and maintained by Molekin slaves.

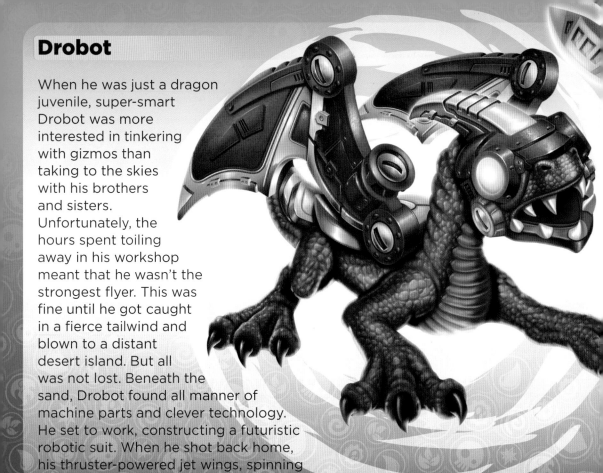

Drobot

When he was just a dragon juvenile, super-smart Drobot was more interested in tinkering with gizmos than taking to the skies with his brothers and sisters. Unfortunately, the hours spent toiling away in his workshop meant that he wasn't the strongest flyer. This was fine until he got caught in a fierce tailwind and blown to a distant desert island. But all was not lost. Beneath the sand, Drobot found all manner of machine parts and clever technology. He set to work, constructing a futuristic robotic suit. When he shot back home, his thruster-powered jet wings, spinning uranium blade gears and sizzling laser beams amazed his fellow dragons. Not only was he the smartest dragon in the sky, he was now the fastest, strongest and most powerful. Thrilled with his new abilities, Drobot sought out Eon, offering his super-charged services as a Skylander.

Drow

Elves that have turned away from the light and embraced a life of Darkness. While they largely work for Kaos, they have retained their elven love of nature – and will defend it to their last enchanted breath.

Drow Archer

An impish archer that sends a flurry of arrows raining down on enemies. Uses Chompies for target practice on days off.

Drow Lance Master

Your basic black-hearted Drow foot-soldier. Drow Lance Masters are perfectionists when it comes to battle. If they miss, the pointy-eared spearmen will pause to give themselves a stinging critique, unwittingly giving their opponent the opportunity to fight back.

Ee

Earth

Do we really need to explain what this is? The very planet you're sitting on. After destroying the Core of Light, Kaos transformed the Skylanders into small toy-like statues and banished them to this small blue and green planet. Luckily, they were discovered by a young Portal Master – you!

Earth Element

One of the main magical Elements of Skylands. All Earth Skylanders have some level of mastery over rock or precious stones.

Earth Spell Punks

Spell Punks who can magic up armor for their allies.

Elements

Eight ancient Elements grant Skylanders their unique powers: Fire, Water, Earth, Air, Life, Undead, Magic and Tech. Some scholars, such as Professor P Grungally, suggest that there are other Elements out there, still waiting to be discovered.

Elves

Green-skinned forest dwellers, elves often work with wood and natural materials. They make formidable warriors.

En Fuego Chompies

Think Chompies but red hot. Not cool.

A B C D E F G H I J K L M N O P Q R S T U V W X Y Z

It was at this moment Eon discovered that he too was a Portal Master. Accidentally activating the Portal, Eon transported Nattybumpo into the middle of the Dirt Seas. Luckily, the wise old man saw the funny side and, after washing the sand out of his beard, taught Eon how to master his magical powers.

Eon went on to protect the Core of Light for centuries, recruiting some of the greatest Skylanders ever known to fight the forces of Darkness. At the end of his life, when his powers

Eon

The greatest Portal Master of all time. When he was a lad, Eon worked as a kitchen hand for a Portal Master by the name of Nattybumpo. Eon was so good at polishing pots and pans that Nattybumpo asked the young boy to give his Portal of Power a quick dust.

Ermit

Instantly recognizable thanks to his nose ring and permanently worried expression, Ermit the Hermit lives in Rumbletown. Why so worried? Well, Ermit believes that the clouds are out to get him.

In truth, Ermit isn't actually a hermit at all. He quite likes people, but spends so much time hiding under a table whenever he sees a cloud that his neighbours mistake his abject terror for a desire to be left alone.

were weakening, Kaos managed to defeat the Skylanders and destroy the Core of Light. Eon was believed dead but had just transmuted himself into spirit form. He now trains the next generation of Skylanders and advises them from beyond the astral plane.

Eruptor

Like all lava beasts, Eruptor was born in the sizzling lava lakes beneath a floating volcanic island. Naturally hot-headed, the molten creatures often argued, especially when enjoying lava pool parties. At one particularly explosive gathering, temperatures flared so much that the entire island erupted. The lava beasts were blasted across the four corners of Skylands, causing raging infernos wherever they landed.

But the cold air had a calming influence on Eruptor. For the first time in his life he relaxed, becoming cool, calm and collected – well, at least compared to his lava-brothers. Now a loyal member of the Skylanders, Eruptor still blows his top every so often and doesn't suffer fools gladly. He's also prone to indigestion, so the other Skylanders keep out of his way whenever he burps up a pool of molten lava.

Eternal Sources

The eight main components of the Core of Light, each linked to an Element. When the Core was destroyed, the Sources were scattered across Skylands.

Evil Eruptor

A nasty version of
the Fire Skylander,
created by Kaos to use
in surprise attacks.

Eye-Brawl

Proof that two Giants are better than one.
Thousands of years ago, a huge flying
eyeball challenged a headless Giant

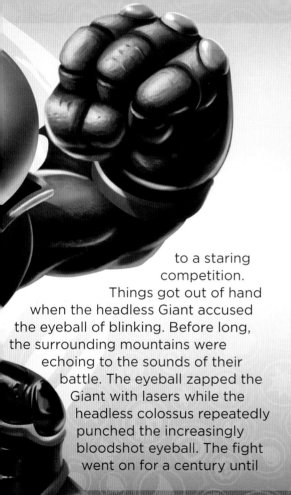

the two combatants finally realized that they were too evenly matched. In fact, they said, imagine how powerful they would be if they joined forces? The eyeball flew onto the Giant's shoulders and Eye-Brawl was born. Before too long, the newly-formed Eye-Brawl joined the Skylanders and set off to defeat the evil Arkeyan King.

Eye-Small

Eye-Brawl's diddy Sidekick. He may be little, but he's always ready to watch the Giant's back.

to a staring competition. Things got out of hand when the headless Giant accused the eyeball of blinking. Before long, the surrounding mountains were echoing to the sounds of their battle. The eyeball zapped the Giant with lasers while the headless colossus repeatedly punched the increasingly bloodshot eyeball. The fight went on for a century until

Ff

Fairies

Fairy folk have long been friends of the Skylanders, largely due to their ability to convert gold and treasure into powerful upgrade spells.

Falling Forest

An area of the Tree of Life. It was largely chopped down by a legion of Kaos' lumberjack trolls searching for the Eternal Life Source. The Core component had been disguised as a huge acorn by the tree folk.

Fire Element

One of the eight main Elements. Fire Skylanders are impervious to lava flows and can survive extreme heat.

Fire Spell Punks

Spell Punks who can detonate dynamite from a distance.

Fat Belly Spider

The yuckiest of all Skylands spiders. Fat Belly Spiders store sticky green goo in their guts, ready to spit at prey. As thrifty as they are terrifying, the emerald nasties suck any unused gunk back into their bellies to use on their next victims. Waste not, want not.

Five Dollars

The amount of cash Kaos owes Terrafin. The skinflint still hasn't paid up.

Flame Imps

Small infernal pests who whip their victims with a red-hot tail. The most stupid of imps, Flamers sometimes try to eat their own feet, only stopping because they burn their own tongues.

Flameslinger

Flameslinger is an elf born with a rare talent. He is able to 'see' through any fire, no matter how near or far. Even when he was a toddler, pilgrims would come from all over Skylands to marvel at his blazing eyes. Before long, his parents even started to sell tickets to gaze into his nursery. Sick of all the attention, Flameslinger tied a blindfold around his enchanted eyes and ran away from home. Alone in the forest, he fashioned himself a bow and practised blindfolded archery, using bomb fiends as movable targets.

Then one evening, as he was about to settle down beneath the stars, he was hit by a vision. Not far away, in a nearby lake, a fire spirit was in trouble. Flameslinger sprinted to the spirit's side, scooping the Elemental out of the water that threatened to extinguish it forever. Burning with gratitude, the fire

spirit gave Flameslinger two gifts – a magical bow that shot blazing arrows, and a pair of boots that enabled him to run at blistering speeds. It urged the young elf to use his gifts wisely and sent Flameslinger in the direction of Master Eon. The far-sighted elf no longer loathes the spotlight and, when he's not protecting Skylands, blazes his way through archery championships.

Flashwing

Flashwing's origins are as mysterious as she is beautiful. She first arrived in Skylands when Bash was staring up at the sky and wishing that he could fly. Suddenly, a falling star streaked across the heavens and smashed into the next valley. Taking it as a sign, Bash rolled to the crash site. There, in the middle of a scorched crater, he found a large crystal egg. His eyes widened as the gem cracked open and Flashwing burst out, unfurling her dazzling wings for the first time.
Bash fell head-over-spiky-clubbed-tail in love with the

gorgeous gem dragon and stumbled forward, blinded by her glittering scales. Sadly, Flashwing mistook the rock dragon for an enemy and blasted him out of the crater with a pulse of blazing laser light from her tail. So, in a funny way, Bash was granted his wish to fly after all.

Today the two dragons often fight side by side, with Flashwing pulling off brilliant attacks that shower her enemies in crystal shards.

Flavius

A dragon knight of Dragon's Peak. Brave but not always bright, Flavius once persuaded Ramses the Dragon King to stretch his wings. Big mistake. Vathek, Ramses' evil brother, used the opportunity to seize the Dragon Throne. Consumed with guilt, Flavius appealed to the Skylanders for help and, while Vathek was distracted, claimed the throne for himself. After using the power of the throne to turn Vathek into stone, Flavius graciously surrendered the throne to Ramses once again. Touched by the red dragon's loyalty, Ramses decided there and then that Flavius would one day rule the kingdom.

Flynn

Flynn is Skylands' greatest pilot – at least, that's what he tells everyone. Taking over-confidence to a new level, Flynn is convinced that he's the right Mabu for the job, even when he obviously isn't. A skilled pilot (even though he's crashed a suspiciously large number of times), Flynn is also quick to take the credit for just about everything and is under the impression that women find him irresistible. Unfortunately, his one true love, Cali, seems more than capable of resisting his advances. Almost as full of hot air as one of his balloons, Flynn isn't as shallow as he first appears. When his friends need him, the conceited captain is always ready to fly head-first into peril. Boom!

Food

Saving Skylands is hungry business. Skylanders need to keep their strength up and always keep an eye out for energy-restoring food that is magically scattered across the islands. Some say the snacks come direct from Eon's own larder, but whatever the source they're always welcome.

Fright Rider

For years, Fright Rider and his spectacular ostrich steed Ozzy thrilled elves by dominating the Skylands Jousting Championships. But on the eve of the 476th contest, a jealous competitor paid a Drow Witch to cast a dark spell. Fright Rider was transported from his tent to the heart of the Land of the Undead. Missing his partner, the naturally nervous Ozzy ate an entire bag of enchanted skele-oats and was transmogrified into a living skeleton. Once transformed, he could storm into the underworld and rescue his companion from a ghoulish fate. After a perilous journey they returned, forever changed but committed to defend those threatened by dark magic. In honour of their bravery they were made Skylanders – but still find time to joust on occasional weekends.

Gg

Gargantulas

Six-legged monster spiders that lasso victims with webbing and then reel them in to feed. And it doesn't get any safer even after they are defeated. Once a Gargantula dies, her body bursts to unleash scuttling Spider Swarmers. Cali will never admit it, but Gargantulas give her the heebie-jeebies.

General Robot

Head of the Robot Army and father to Clam-Tron 4000. He enlisted the help of the Skylanders after his robo-troops were outnumbered by the trolls guarding the Core of Light's Golden Gear. Pastimes include polishing his medals and kicking stinky troll behind. However, for all his tough talk, the mechanical military man is scared clogless by anything remotely supernatural.

Glacier Gully

Believing that his massive Arkeyan robot was haunted, Ermit the Hermit dumped the 'bot in the icy wastes of Glacier Gully. The local Ice Ogres mistook the frozen machine for their Great Evil Ice Master and left sacrifices of ice blocks and snowmen at its dormant feet.

Ghosts

Like the majority of undead souls, the spectres of Skylands feasted on the living until they tasted Batterson's delicious pies.

Ghost Pirate Swords

Magical items that can be used by the Skylanders. The Ghost Pirate Swords summon two whirling spectral sabres that follow the champion around and attack enemies.

Glowing Green Goo of Primordia

The gloopy green substance that oils the Golden Gears of the Core of Life. After years of not being that great with technology, the trolls made a massive leap forward when they discovered the secrets of the goo.

Ghost Roaster

Ghost Roaster didn't ask to be a ghoul. Once upon a time, he was but a humble chef by the name of Olav. He lived high on a mountain and loved to cook, especially his speciality, sheep-wool stew. It was while foraging for wool that the accident happened. He spotted a rare purple sheep standing on a cliff. Knowing how great that purple wool would taste, he climbed the side of the mountain and inched towards the oblivious creature. Suddenly, a gust of wind blew Olav over the edge. He tumbled head over heels down the mountain, landing in a heap at the bottom. But a few aches and bruises were the least of his worries. He had fallen into the Valley of the Undead and had been transformed into a hideous, skull-faced ghoul. Even worse, he had an insatiable hunger for ghosts!

Calling himself Ghost Roaster, the cursed chef ploughed through undead villages, chewing up entire phantom populations. Eventually he was captured by the local ethereal ruler. The enraged royal chained Roaster to a spiked ball that rattled to warn startled spooks. Eon took pity on the malnourished monster and made Ghost Roaster a Skylander – but only after he promised not to gorge on any more ghosties!

Giant Floating Head

To make up for his short physical stature, Kaos often projects a massive spectral version of his head over Skylands. Only marginally more frightening than Kaos' own noggin, his Giant Floating Head does have the benefit of not smelling as bad as the real thing.

Gigantus

A huge, moss-covered Rock Golem from the time of the Arkeyan Empire. He lived in the Ancient Mines and spent his days jumping through holes. Then, one day, he leapt through a cracked flagstone and was never seen again.

Giants

The original Skylanders. 10,000 years ago, the Giants formed a robot-bashing group to rid Skylands of the Arkeyans once and for all. They defeated the Arkeyan King but were banished to Earth, where they were discovered by young human Portal Masters.

Gill Grunt

Even as a tiddler Gill wanted to be in the Gillmen Marines. He used to sit at his window staring out into the murky depths, imagining the adventures he would have. Enlisted as soon as he graduated from fish school, Gill rose through the ranks to become the bravest Marine of them all. The best shot that the Gillmen High Command had ever seen, Gill was expected to become the youngest general in Marine history. But his head was turned when

manoeuvres took him to a misty lagoon island in the sky. As he swept the jungle for spit spiders he heard someone singing gently on the breeze. Following the song, his heart flipped when he came face to fin with the most beautiful mermaid he'd ever seen. The Marine and the siren fell instantly in love, and Gill promised to return to her after his next tour of duty. Sadly, when he finally made it back to the lagoon, he discovered that his beloved had been fin-napped by a crew of pesky pirates. Quitting the Marines, he set out to find his fishtailed love, searching high and low, but she was nowhere to be seen. Master Eon took pity on the heartbroken hero and welcomed him into the Skylanders. Now, Gill serves Skylands while continuing to keep an ear out for the sound of a familiar mermaid's song drifting over the sea.

81

Gillmen Marines

Crack underwater commandos who protect Skylands' many seas. Their motto is 'He Who Dares, Swims'.

Gill Runt

Gill Grunt's tiddly Sidekick. Loves hanging out with his aquatic hero.

Glumshanks

You have to feel sorry for Kaos' right-hand troll. Not only is he bound to fulfil the evil Portal Master's every demand, he also has to wash Kaos' stinking socks. Eurgh!

Glumshanks was butler to Kaos' family when the little twerp was growing up and has stuck by his Master ever since. When Kaos was defeated by the Skylanders and exiled to Earth as a toy, Glumshanks searched the cosmos for his Lord, eventually finding him in a Super Toy Planet store. Not that Kaos thanked his most faithful servant of course – he never does.

Golden Gear, the

The vital cog of the Core of Light that keeps the universe ticking along.

Gnashers

If you thought Fire Imps were hot, you ain't seen nothing yet. Their scorching blue cousins are hot enough to melt Kaos' stinky socks.

Goliath Drow

Tall, green and gruesome, the muscle-bound Goliath Drow are the heavies of Skylands. Armed with two spiky shields, they can move remarkably quickly for their size. Nothing can stop a Goliath when it's in full charge.

Good King Roland

The beloved ruler of the great Crustacean Kingdom and father of Wham-Shell. Wise old Roland reigned peacefully for hundreds of years until his territory was invaded by oil-drilling trolls.

Griffins

Winged creatures that live high in the mountains of Skylands. Evil wizards will risk life and limb to steal griffin eggs from their nests.

Grenade Generals

The terror of the troll battlefield, giggling Grenade Generals stand behind the lines, lobbing timed explosives into the melee. A little known fact is that Grenade Generals never remove their spiked helmets. Not even when they go to bed.

Gurglefin

A Gillman and long-time friend of the Skylanders. Despite an aversion to danger, Gurglefin has always wanted to be a pirate – just don't tell Gill Grunt!

Hh

Hair Tonic

Many moons ago, all Molekin boasted long flowing locks. However, a troll trickster persuaded them that crude oil made fantastic hair tonic. The duped miners lathered their heads in the stuff and all their hair fell out. Now all Molekin are bald and oil is just used in machines.

Haldor

Haldor, the Great Northern Wizard, appealed to the Skylanders for help after Ice Ogres blocked off the sun and turned the village of Vindlevale into a frozen wasteland. Brrrr.

Hats

Skylanders love hats, and for good reason. Not only do they make you look great, they can also boost your natural abilities. Magic hats are to be found hidden all over Skylands, packed in special hatboxes. The one hat no one wants to find is the compost heap cap. It makes its wearer smell worse than a cyclops eating rotten egg sandwiches.

Hatterson

Batterson's baby brother and the maker of the finest enchanted hats in all of Skylands.

Healing Elixir

One of the magical items of Skylands. Just a drop of its life-giving juice will restore you to full vigour.

Hektore

A fearsome invader from the Outlands. Hektore was granted terrible powers by the Darkness and enslaved the Mystic Seekers of the Radiant Isles. He forced the Seekers to build the Dark Mirror that shrouded his foul deeds from the rest of Skylands. Defeated by the Skylanders, Hektore was destroyed when the Dark Mirror shattered.

Heroic Challenges

Part of the Skylanders' training process. Cali helps each champion explore their powers by sending them across Skylands to complete a series of challenges.

Hex

A gifted sorceress, Hex was admired throughout Skylands. News of her abilities even reached Malefor, the Undead Dragon King and lord of the Underworld. Wanting her power for himself, Malefor commanded that his minions bring the witch to his throne room. His dragon horde scoured the country, burning village after village. But Hex's fellow wizards weren't about to give her up. Bravely, they placed the sorceress in hiding and took on the dragons themselves. Hex couldn't stand to see her

brothers and sisters in magic sacrifice themselves and so took the fight to Malefor, storming the Underworld herself. She battled through Shadow Knights, Rhu-Barbs and hideous Undead Golems until she faced the Dragon King himself. Casting a terrible spell, Hex turned Malefor's own dark magic against him, destroying his lair in a flash of blinding blackness. When the smoke cleared, she found herself back in her village, but her journey had come at a price – she had joined the ranks of the Undead. Pledging to always protect magic-wielders from evil, Hex became a Skylander. Able to summon a rain of screaming skulls, Hex is feared across Skylands, although Eon knows that the mysterious spell-caster is one of his most trustworthy warriors.

Hob 'n' Yaro

A master thief who will steal anything that isn't nailed down. Actually, thinking about it, he would probably still have a go and then nick the nails too!

Hot Air Balloons

Unable to use Portals, most Skylands citizens travel from island to island using Hot Air Balloons. The Drow claim to have invented Hot Air Balloons but this isn't true. It was actually a Chompy. The greedy little critter drank 200 flasks of fizzy juice, swelled to three times its normal size and then floated away, burping like mad!

back to earth in the middle of a Skylander camp, immediately setting Gill Grunt's tent on fire. Gill's ruined tent was soon forgotten as Hot Dog saved his new friends from the clutches of a Lava Golem, an act of bravery that saw the brave pooch made a sizzling Skylander. Hot Dog promptly made himself at home in the Citadel by burying Eon's mystic staff.

Hot Head

When he heard that a new magical oil had been discovered, short-tempered Hot Head just had to see it for himself. The Fire Giant hotfooted it to the black lagoon and gaped in wonder at the sea of enchanted ebony. In fact, he was so overcome by the excitement that he jumped right in. Whoops. The oil exploded, totally destroying the island. While it would be another two centuries before a

Hot Dog

A molten mutt who can bark up balls of fire, Hot Dog was born in the belly of the Popcorn Volcano. Shot into the air when the mountain unexpectedly erupted, the pyro-pup came crashing

natural spring of the magic oil was rediscovered, the strange goo had a profound effect on Hot Head. It now pulsed through his red-hot veins, allowing him to burn brighter than ever. Now able to shoot columns of fire or blazing oil slicks from his hands, Hot Head joined the other Giants to fight the evil Arkeyans.

Humfry

The most powerful – and grumpy – of the Mystic Seekers.

Hydra

Arguably the most powerful of Kaos' minions. This four-headed beast

Hugo

This nervous little Mabu is Master Eon's chief assistant, librarian and resident historian. Always found with his nose stuck in a book, Hugo is a font of knowledge but isn't the bravest fellow in Skylands. Above all, Hugo is inexplicably terrified of sheep. No matter how much Eon tries to convince him to the contrary, hapless Hugo believes that the woolly creatures are planning to take over the world.

Ice Ogres

managed to destroy the Core of Light, allowing Darkness to flood into Skylands. Each of its heads belonged to a different Element. The Fire head spewed roving fireballs and summoned micro-volcanoes, while the Life head controlled red energy-chomping bugs. The Undead head could conjure deadly laser beams while the Water head brought tsunamis of doomshark-infested waters. When Kaos was finally defeated, the Hydra retreated into the Darkness where it lies in wait to strike once again.

Abominable snowmen who may be as thick as a block of ice but are still a force to be reckoned with. Even though they're cold-hearted through and through, their fire-breathing magic staffs soon heat things up.

Ignitor

Poor old Ignatius. The inexperienced knight grew up in a land terrorized by a vicious red dragon. Eager to bring an end to his people's plight, he pulled on his tattered armor and clunked off for the toughest duel of his young life. On the way, he met a witch who offered him a gift that seemed too good to be true (and, in fact, was). She equipped him with an enchanted suit of armor that would help him slay the beast – but it came at a terrible price. Despite defeating the dragon, he found himself transformed into a fire spirit, forever doomed to burn inside the accursed armor. But all was not lost. Taking the name Ignitor, he joined the Skylanders. Now the spirited knight defends the honour of Skylands while keeping an eye out for the witch who tricked him all those years ago.

Inhuman Shields

With their gruesome shields held high, these uncanny knights are completely impervious to attack from the front. Only a surprise beating from behind will bring them down, but be careful they don't strike a spinning blow first.

Iron Fist of Arkus, the

The source of the Ancient Arkeyans' power. Once the Iron Fist was ripped from the Arkeyan King's arm, his robot army sank into a powerless sleep. 10,000 years later, Kaos discovered the Iron Fist and was transformed into a giant War Machine and Emperor of the New Arkeyan Empire. Finally, he had a body as big as his ego. Nearly.

Islands

An infinite number of islands float through Skylands' rolling clouds. Some are peaceful and some are petrifying, but all are springboards to adventure.

Jj

Jawbreakers

Beastly – if clumsy – bruisers who love a good scrap. While they have a mean right hook (and a nasty left one too) they often trip over their own feet.

Jess LeGrand

The plucky daughter of Mayor LeGrand summoned the Skylanders after Captain Dreadbeard's marauding crew invaded Plunder Island. After Dreadbeard was defeated, the scurvy wretch captured Jess and dragged her back to his lair. Luckily, the Skylanders were hot on his heels.

Jet-Vac

The most daring flying ace in all of Windham, Jet-Vac received his magical wings when he was still in the nest. When Windham came under attack years later, the Sky Baron gave his wings to a young mother so that she could fly her children out of danger. Doomed never to take to the skies again, Jet-Vac fought bravely on and was soon noticed by Eon. Impressed by his self-sacrifice, Eon gave Jet-Vac a powerful vacuum cannon – The Vac Blaster 9000. Not only could the weapon blast enemies with compressed air, it also allowed the eagle-eyed Sky Baron to soar through the clouds once again. Now a trusted Skylander, Jet-Vac leads aerial assaults on Kaos and his minions.

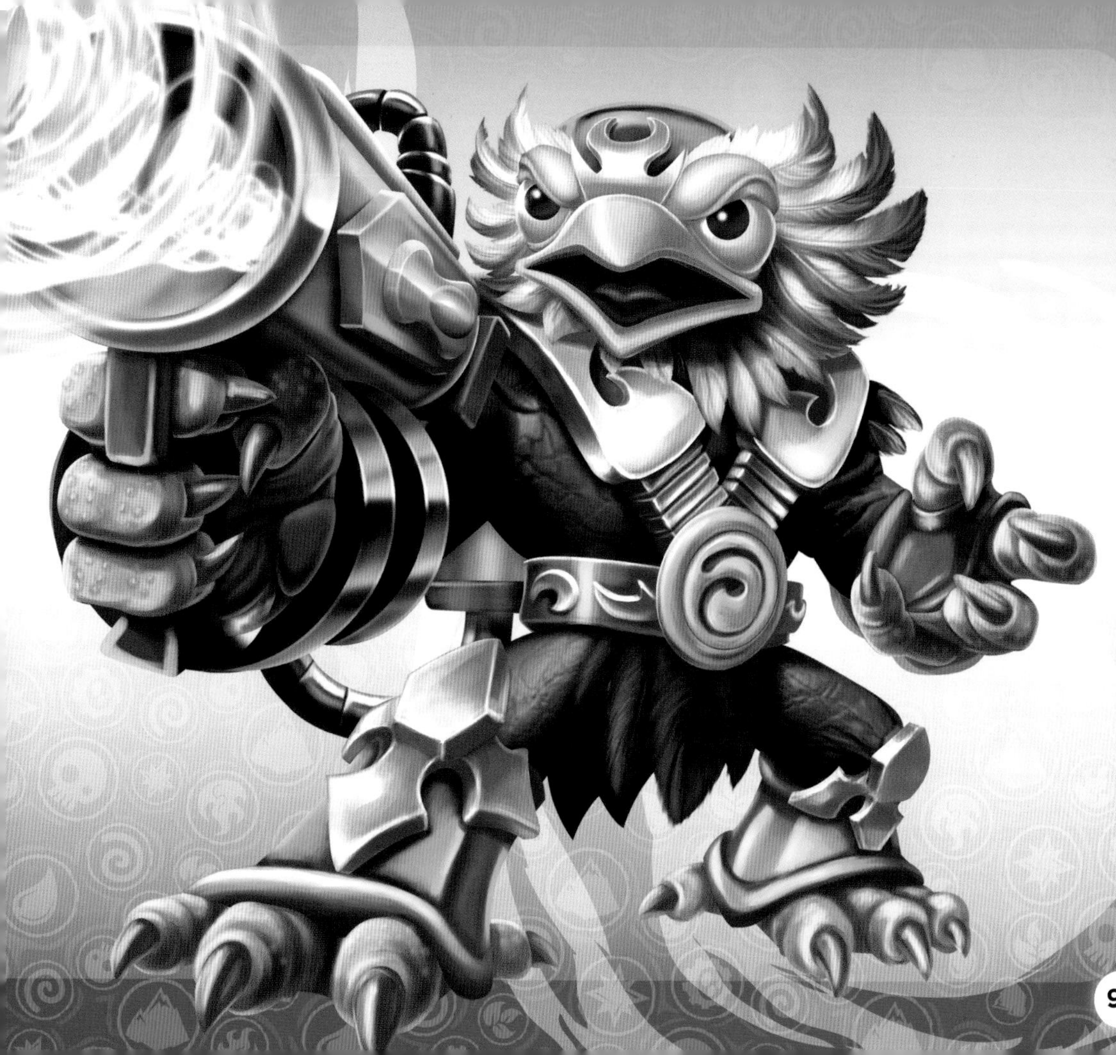

Kk

Kaos

The most evil Portal Master ever to exist, Kaos thinks only of power and universal domination. He has tried to take over Skylands more times than even the greediest gut-golem has had hot dinners – which is a lot. His first attempt was probably the sneakiest. He had statues of himself erected all over Skylands in the hope that people would just assume that he was their king. When that didn't work, he resorted to more nefarious means.

Even though he is small, ugly and very, very smelly, Kaos should never be underestimated. He is a powerful wizard and has never given up, even when he was banished to the remote Outlands by Eon. Incredibly fond of his

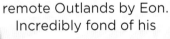

Giant Floating Head (which he insists you should all fear, by the way) he has gathered an army of minions and is constantly accompanied by his butler-turned-henchtroll, Glumshanks.

Whether his mania is the product of an unhappy childhood is unknown. We do know that he was so lonely as a child that he was forced to create an artificial life form – the wooden Wilikins – to play with. Later, as a spotty teenager, he would heap treasure into piles on the balconies of his castle, pretend they were beautiful princesses and sing love songs to them. All rather pathetic really.

Kaos' Kastle

The ancestral seat of the Kaos family. After his floating lair was destroyed by the Skylanders, the evil Portal Master returned to his birthplace. Full of unknown riches and devious traps, the Kastle once boasted a rather wonderful pool. Unfortunately, Kaos was forced to have it drained as too many of his troll guards were toppling into the water. Trolls can't swim, you see.

Ll

Lava Kings

Evil blobs of molten madness that will get you hot under the collar. Get too close and they will spit sizzling Flame Imps at you. What a disgusting habit.

Lava Lakes Railway

The most sweltering train journey you will ever take. Diggs the Molekin once helped to get the Lava Lakes Express going while the Skylanders searched for the Eternal Fire Source. Choo choo!

Legendary Treasures

There's a reason that treasure hunters love exploring Skylands. The place is absolutely bursting with treasure hidden here, there and everywhere. Some Legendary Treasures can even be used to upgrade The Dread-Yacht, which is fortunate, as Flynn's flying bucket of bolts is constantly falling apart.

Leveler, the

The greatest catapult ever built. The Leveler defended the balmy valley of Vindlevale for hundreds of years against the threat posed by the Ice Ogres of the nearby snowy mountains.

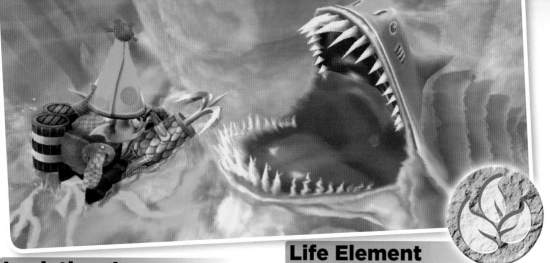

Leviathan Lagoon

Leviathan Lagoon is a pleasant shrine-filled realm of warm seas and tropical islands, the perfect holiday spot – if it wasn't for the gargantuan killer fish that devours entire villages. An ideal place to hide the Eternal Water Source, then.

Life Element

One of the main magical Elements that surge through Skylands. Life Skylanders have mastery over the natural world.

Life Spell Punks

Spell Punks with strange healing powers.

Lightning Rod

The most macho of all the Storm Titans, Lightning Rod dominated every Storm Games for centuries. The walls of the All-Weather Arena were bustling with statues of the blue-skinned sports hero, and with good reason. As his best-selling autobiography 'Rod the Bod' reports, he was the master of the 250-ton bench press, undisputed champion of the lightning-fast cloud sprint, and top of the table of the 1,000-metre lightning bolt hurl. After an eternity of adulation, Rod

was getting bored of being brilliant. Thankfully, his life changed when, during the Triple Gold Ring Lightning Bolt Toss (With a Twist), Kaos' giant floating head appeared in the clouds above the arena. The horrid Portal Master demanded that the Titans submit to his will, and Rod answered on their behalf by blasting Kaos out of the sky. The crowd went wild, including Eon who was a guest of the Storm King. Eon offered Rod the chance to become a Skylander, and the electrifying Titan immediately accepted.

Lost City of Arkus

The majestic underground capital city of the ancient Arkeyan Empire, lost for 10,000 years and then found by Kaos. Why was it lost in the first place? Well, as previously mentioned, Arkeyans had terrible trouble remembering anything buried beneath them. Why they decided to build their greatest city beneath the ground is anyone's guess.

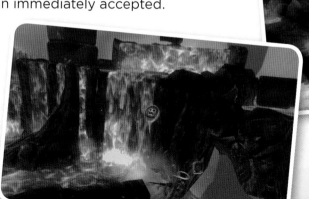

Mm

Small, fuzzy and meek, the Mabu haven't got a mean bone in their bodies. They do, however, have far-too-trusting, prone-to-getting-in-trouble and most-likely-to-be-enslaved bones in their left wrists.

Mabu

One of the most common creatures found in Skylands.

Mabu Defense Force, the

Formed to defend Mabu villages from the encroaching troll menace. Founded by former florist Rizzo, and commanded by General Robot, the MDF meant well but was largely rubbish.

Mace Majors

Troll Greasemonkeys who have greased their way up the ranks and been rewarded with heavy, spiked maces.

Machine Ghost

A friendly spirit that haunted Ermit's Arkeyan War Machine. Machine Ghost so terrified the hermit that Ermit dumped the huge robot in Glacier Gully, trapping the spectre in the ice. After being rescued by the Skylanders, Machine Ghost helped defeat Kaos by wrestling the evil Portal Master's robot form.

Malacostracan Mace

The mystic staff of the Crustacean Kingdom, passed down from one king to another. Now wielded by Wham-Shell.

Malefor

The Undead Dragon King of the Underworld. Banished from Skylands by Hex during a spirited battle.

Magic Element

The very essence of Skylands. Magic flows through every island, every rock, every tree, every beast – yes even every sheep. Of all the Eternal Sources, the Magic Source is the most powerful. After the Core was destroyed, the source fell back through time and was locked away in the vault of the great Arkeyan Temple. Corrupt though they may have been, the Arkeyans knew what would happen if it fell into the wrong hands.

Magic Spell Punks

Spell Punks who blast bolts of pure magic.

Mermaids

Half human, half fish, Mermaids spend most of their days sitting on rocks, combing their hair and having people fall in love with them. Sounds like hard work. Not.

Mini-Jini

Ninjini's mystical, magical sidekick.

Mohawk Cyclops

After years of being bald, cyclops warriors got fed up of being teased, so stuck on punky hairstyles using Slobbering Mutticus spit. Their new hairdos didn't help their fighting abilities though. The clumsy cyclopses insist on spinning into battles, while simultaneously waving giant axes around, even though it makes them unbelievably dizzy.

Mole Drop

A curious Molekin custom. The shortsighted miners often yell 'Mole Drop' and leap down their neighbours' chimneys. The resident of the house then awards the Mole Dropper marks out of six, based on how surprised they are.

Molekin

A friendly race of visually impaired miners. Centuries ago, the Molekin won the contract for any construction work on Skylands. Unfortunately, due to their poor eyesight they didn't read the small print. This means they must accept work from anyone who demands it, be they good or deranged evil overlords. Oops.

Mortalannis

Philosopher King and First Lord of the Undead. Was also said to wear a rather unconvincing bone wig.

Mystic Seekers

A band of spiritual Mabu who harvest the mystical energies of the Radiance on Radiant Isles. Led by Fargus, they were forced to create the Dark Mirror by the evil Hektore.

Nn

Nattybumpo

The Portal Master who taught Eon everything he knew. Nattybumpo had the largest, reddest, bushiest beard you ever could see. It was so large that birds used to nest in it every spring.

Nauteloids

Blade-beaked ducks who lurk around beaches waiting to inconvenience sunbathers.

Noodles

An idiotic Ice Ogre who worshipped the 'Great Evil Ice Master'. As a child, Noodles tried to catch hailstones on his tongue. Unfortunately, as most hailstones in Glacier Gully are the size of footballs, he spent most of his youth with severe concussion. He never really recovered.

Nort

Hailing from Shattered Island, Nort became a scout for the Mabu Defense Force.

Ninjini

Millennia before the corrupt Arkeyan Empire spread across Skylands, Ninjini was the realm's number one magical ninja. This drove the number two magical ninja green with jealousy (actually, as an elf, the envious sorceress was already green, but you get the idea).

Conjuring dark magic, the wicked wannabe trapped Ninjini inside an enchanted bottle, where she was cursed to remain for eternity.

However, Ninjini refused to let her imprisonment get her down. She used her solitude as a chance to practise both her magic and dual sword techniques. As the centuries dragged by, Ninjini grew in power – and size – eventually cracking the bottle. She pushed herself free and, hearing about the plight of Skylands in the face of the Arkeyan menace, became one of the very first Skylanders. She still carries her enchanted bottle with her to remind her to never, ever surrender.

Oo

Octophonic Music Player

A magical musical device salvaged by Flynn from Junkyard Isles. It is said to be able to play any tune ever composed, but thanks to the Dread-Yacht's curse it keeps getting stuck.

Occulous

Basically a massive floating eyeball, with added fronds! Occulous crowned himself King of the Undead and banned everyone from buying Batterson's pies. He was eventually banished by the Skylanders, plopping into Darklight Crypt's murky moat. It's worth keeping an eye out for Occulous though. He could blink back into existence at any moment.

Oilspill Island

A peaceful harbour until the trolls conquered the island and started drilling for oil.

Onk Beakman

Skylands' best-selling author. This book-loving penguin wrote his first novel before he was even hatched (although where he got the paper and pencil from while still in his egg remains a mystery). Growing up in Skylands' Frozen Desert, Onk soon discovered that he hated the cold, so lost himself in stories of warmer climes. Unbeknownst to the Beakman family, their two-storey igloo home was built on the site of a buried super-weapon from the dawn of time. They couldn't have been more surprised when Kaos appeared and tried to melt the icebergs to get at the doomsday device. Onk was saved by Spyro, who flew in and blasted Kaos back to his lair. From that day forward, Onk vowed to travel to every island in Skylands, collecting stories

of the brave Skylanders. He now lives on Blistering Beach with his two pet sea-cucumbers, Squirt and Squiggle.

Ooga Orcs

Once the fiercest fighters in Skylands, the Ooga Orc tribe bravely marched off to face the Darkness in battle. Only Voodood returned alive.

Oracle, the

The Oracle, or Octavius Cloptimus, is a one-eyed, multi-tentacled creature who exists just outside the boundaries of time and space. The Oracle can see into the past, and to some degree the present, but not the future. Yet. Let's just say it's a work in progress. To help his research, Octavius sets tasks for his visitors. By studying the choices he makes, the Oracle hopes to unlock the secrets of years to come. He is certainly on the right path. For example, he's predicted that the next entry in this A-Z would be Perilous Pastures. Let's see if he's right . . .

Pp

Perilous Pastures

The last resting place of the mysterious Enigma Pig, one of Skyland's rarest Legendary Treasures. It was from here that the Skylanders rescued Cali from a coven of evil Drow.

Persephone

A long-time friend of the Skylanders, Persephone the fairy provides Eon's champions with power upgrades in return for treasure. She's always flitting around, perhaps to avoid Flynn's awful chat-up lines.

Pipsqueak

A puny cyclops lord. Pipsqueak and his cronies invaded Molekin Mountain, setting up a gaming arena much to the Molekin's dismay. As weak as he is chinless, Pipsqueak only crawled up the cyclops social ladder thanks to a bevy of influential one-eyed uncles.

worse. Stale sheep-wool biscuits, anyone? Yuk! No wonder they distract themselves by playing Pirate Cards and Skystones at every opportunity. Yarr!

Poop Deck

One of the pirates' greatest secrets. Just what is a poop deck? Best not to ask, really, just in case they make you swab it. Shudder.

Pirates

The terror of Skylands' seas – and skies. It's tough being a pirate. Yes, there is all the pillaging and plundering, but the hours are terrible and the food even

Popcorn Mountain

Hot Dog's volcanic birthplace. Nothing grows on its scorched faces, except for the mega-rare Exploding Popcorn Plant. To pass the time, young lava beasts try to cram as many seeds from the plant into their mouths as possible before the pods erupt in a shower of sparks.

Pop Fizz

Pop Fizz is not the alchemist he was. In fact, he doesn't even know who – or what – he was before he started experimenting with magical potions. His appearance, colour and even voice have changed beyond belief over the years. All that is known for sure is that Pop's a little crazy. Actually, scratch that – he's a lot crazy.

Most of his demented chemical experiments end in an explosion – or him being transformed into goodness knows what. This recklessness meant that for most of his life folk stayed clear of him, so the cuckoo chemist started brewing a potion that he hoped would change all that. It didn't exactly go to plan. Instead of making him charming and irresistible, his super-soda just turned him into a wild and woolly beastly berserker. Thankfully, Eon saw potential in Pop Fizz's potty potions and invited him – cautiously – to become a Skylander.

Portal Masters

Beings who can manipulate Portals of Power. Portal Masters are born with this ability, although the number of Portal Masters alive at one time has varied across history. At one point it was believed that Eon was the last of the Portal Masters. Then Kaos raised his ugly head (boo!) but was defeated by a new generation of Portal Masters from the planet Earth (hurray!).

Portal of Power

A magical platform that can transport beings to anywhere in the universe. Portals of Power are found all over Skylands but can only be used by a Portal Master. With enough practice they can even be used to travel back in time, which is handy if you've missed someone's birthday.

Prism Break

It's fair to say that Prism Break was a Rock Golem who didn't like being disturbed. All he wanted was to be left alone in his mine home. Unfortunately for the gravelly grump, the walls of his mine were laced with all manner of gems and jewels. No Molekin miner could resist trying to dig out such riches, so Prism spent his days battering underground interlopers and reducing their mining machines to scrap metal. Eventually the miners got the message and Prism Break was left in peace. Shattered from the constant interruptions, the Rock Golem fell asleep. He awoke, over 100 years later, when a Molekin pickaxe struck him in a place he'd rather not discuss. Roaring more in surprise than pain, he discovered he had been trapped in a cave-in. The extreme pressure of hundreds of tons of earth pressing down on him had transformed his rocky arms into shining gems that could project powerful energy beams. Grateful to the Molekin for releasing him, Prism Break pledged to use his new powers for good and thundered off to join the Skylanders.

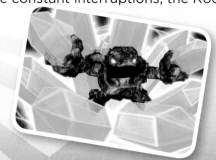

Professor P Grungally

Respected Skylands scholar, hero worshipped by Hugo. Grungally wrote all 2,007 volumes of the seminal 'Rise and Fall of the Ancient Arkeyans'. Hugo thinks they get a bit stale around volume 1,462, but pick up by the end.

119

Qq

Quicksilver Vault

The ancient Arkeyan repository of Quicksilver, a magical metal used to write runes of great power.

Quigley

The son of a royal family of Mabu who originally lived on Shattered Island, not that you'd know it to look at him. The little lad would much rather wear his favourite windmill hat than a golden crown.

Rr

Raccoons

A family of angry raccoons originally powered the Dread-Yacht. However, it wasn't the most efficient propulsion system, so Auric provided Flynn with a brand new super-dooper engine that only breaks down once every three journeys. Well, it's an improvement at least.

Radiance, the

A source of power second only to the Core of Light.

Ramses

The King of Dragon's Peak and the only dragon who has ever grown a beard.

Rhu-Babies

Scythe-armed scuttlers from another dimension. Their pink pincers are in no way cute.

Rhu-Barbs

What do you get if you cross an Undead Spell Punk with a Rhu-Baby? A supersized and super-grizzly Rhu-Barb, that's what.

Rizzo

The former Mabu florist who founded the Mabu Defense Force. Rather fond of pirate hats.

Roboto-Ball

A popular sport on ancient Skylands, made even more thrilling by the fact that Roboto-Balls had a habit of exploding halfway through the game.

Rock Walkers

Two-legged Rock Golems who belch out small pools of lava.

Rocket Imps

Annoying yellow imps that enjoy firing rockets at anyone who comes near.

Root Runners

A new variety of Chompy Pod, able to hoist themselves up on their roots and go for a wander.

Rocker Walkers

These Golems don't spew out lava. Phew! Hang on . . . they spit out fireballs instead? Now that's just rude.

Ruins, the

All that is left of Eon's once spectacular Citadel, which was destroyed when the Core of Light erupted. After the Core was reassembled, Eon's lush gardens returned to their former glory, although the Portal Master's castle remains a shadow of its past self.

Rumbletown

The township once ruled by Brock and home to Ermit the misnamed Hermit. Just watch you don't fall into the Chompy-infested Cavern of Echoing Nibbles!

Rotting Robbies

Zombies from the Underworld, liable to lose limbs at a moment's notice. Can be destroyed by fire – or the careful application of a cannon.

Ss

Seadog Pirates

Canine crooks with very big cutlasses. You can tell they're coming from the reek of wet dog.

Secret Vault of Secrets

A vast underwater vault of Arkeyan wonders hidden behind a series of towering dams at the end of a deep rocky gorge. Here, the Arkeyans kept a map that would help them find the city of Arkus if ever they mislaid it. Which, of course, they did. How careless.

Shadow Dukes

Don't stand around admiring these impressive suits of armor. They're haunted and will try to chop your head off!

Sheep

Dull, grass-munching critters or scheming, tyrannical beasts? You decide.

Shattered Island

Once home to a large population of Mabu, Shattered Island lived up to its name when it was struck by a freak tornado.

Shroomboom

Born in Kaos' pizza-topping patch, fun guy Shroomboom knew that his destiny was to be baked on a bed of cheese and tomato. So he fashioned a catapult from an old twig and a strand of spider silk, and fired his mushroom mates over the garden fence to safety. Narrowly missing being plucked himself,

Shroomboom was the last to launch into the night sky, and gently floated back to the ground using his cap as a parachute. Bravely, he led the terrified toadstools out of Kaos' grounds and away to freedom. The fungal friends found sanctuary at Eon's Citadel, where Shroomboom was made a Life Skylander.

127

Sidekicks

Miniature versions of the Skylanders. Eruptor believes that Double Trouble and Pop Fizz created them during a failed experiment, although the two potion-producers deny all knowledge. Faithful to the end, Sidekicks will follow at the heels of any Skylander when allowed up on to a Portal.

Skitterbooms

See Spider Swarmers.

Sky Barons

The flying aces of Windham. Bizarrely, it is said that male Sky Barons have been known to lay eggs in moments of great stress or surprise.

Sky-Iron Shield

One of Skylands' fabled magical items. The Shield protects its Skylander against attack.

Skylanders

Legendary protectors of Skylands. The Skylanders are gathered together by Portal Masters to defend the Core of Light and fight the forces of Darkness.

Skylands

A magical realm made up of an infinite number of islands floating in a sea of endless clouds. From here, you can jump to any location in the universe, which is why the Skylanders have pledged to protect it from evil. If it ever fell into the wrong hands, nowhere would be safe.

Skystones

The gaming craze that has taken Skylands by storm. It was invented by a lazy group of Molekin tilers. Bored with laying tiles, they made a game out of it, each trying to win as many tiles as possible. Their afternoon diversion became Skystones and the Molekin became so rich on the game's profits that they never had to even look at another tile again.

Sky Schooner Docks

A group of islands patrolled by Drow Zeppelins.

Slam Bam

Slam Bam's life was a happy one. The solitary yeti lived alone on a floating ice glacier, carving ice-sculptures and making delicious snow cones. However, far away, Kaos regarded the four-armed snowman with envious eyes. The Portal Master wanted the secret to Slam Bam's perfect snow cones and, when the yeti refused to give it up, melted the glacier away to nothing. Slam Bam only escaped by jumping onto a passing iceberg. He drifted through Skylands, finally coming to rest on Eon's own island. Eon persuaded the frosty, four-fisted one to become a Skylander, putting evil on ice in his perishing prisons.

Slobbering Mutticus

Horrendous hounds used by cyclopses as monstrous mounts. If their pounding paws don't get you, their sticky slobber will. It's so gooey that cyclops stonemasons use it to stick slabs together.

Smoltergeist

Most ghosts are cold-hearted, but not Smoltergeist. This sizzling spook haunts lava-lakes and flaming forests.

Snowclopses

Another variety of cold-loving cyclopses. Usually found hanging around Ice Ogres (probably because Ice Ogres are the only creatures that make cyclopses look smart!).

Snuckles

The Mabu who raised the alarm when a tornado struck Shattered Island. Snuckles never considered himself brave, but was recruited by General Robot as a top secret agent.

Sodaworks, the

When Kaos was a child, his family used to make their own soda in a factory located deep in Kastle Kaos. Sadly it didn't sell, largely due to the flavours. Seriously, would you want to drink sand, mud or radioactive suction eel-flavoured pop?

Sonic Boom

A naturally protective mother, Sonic Boom chose one of the highest mountains on Skylands to lay her griffin eggs. But even there, she wasn't safe. A shady sorceror, keen to use baby griffin feathers in his spells, climbed to the summit to snatch an egg. Sonic sent him tumbling back down the mountainside with an ear-splitting shriek. But, as he fell to his doom, the vengeful wizard cast a callous curse. Sonic's eggs would hatch, but her

brood would magically return to their shells mere moments later. With them trapped in an eternal time loop, Sonic Boom would never see her children fully grown. The grief-stricken griffin joined the Skylanders, where Eon helped her train her chicks to protect Skylands every time they hatch.

Sparx the Dragonfly

A long-time friend of Spyro, Sparx the Dragonfly often helps Skylanders blast their way through enemy ranks. His flaming spitballs transform bad guys into a dragonfly-sized butterfly snack. Bzzzzzz!

Soul Gems

Glittering purple gems that grant Skylanders amazing new powers. Semi-sentient, they come into being whenever a new Skylander is born and hide themselves away until they are needed the most.

Spell Punks

Mischievous little mages who, instead of using their vast magical powers for good, create havoc wherever they go. Like Skylanders, different Spell Punks belong to different Elements, which bring them slightly different powers. No one knows what they look like beneath those hoods, but many suspect they have pointy heads that go all the way up to the top of their hats.

Spider Swarmers

Diddy spiders that scurry towards their victims, not to bite them, but to blow them up. Also known as Skitterbooms in some parts of Skylands.

Spiderlings

Poisonous baby spiders. Definitely not sweet.

Spider Spitters

White globby sacs that spawn Spider Swarmers. Destroy the sac and you'll stop the flow of scuttling spiders.

Sprocket

Born into a life of privilege, this down-to-earth Golding cared little for treasure or trinkets. Instead, she spent as much time as possible in her uncle's workshop, watching as he built all manner of crazy contraptions. Then one day, her inventive uncle vanished. Discovering that Kaos had snatched him and was forcing him to build dark engines of destruction, Sprocket ventured off on a quest to return her beloved uncle home – a quest that continues to this day. Throwing her lot in with Eon, she joined the Skylanders and now carries on her search as a fully-fledged Skylander.

Spyro

According to Professor P Grungally, the Ancient Scrolls outline Skylands' long history and even longer future. They also chronicle the adventures of the rare purple dragon known as Spyro. The Portal Masters of yore first realized his potential centuries ago, but it was Eon who reached across the boundaries between this and Spyro's own dimension and invited him to become a Skylander. A natural-born leader, Spyro has the ability to channel power from all eight Elements, as well as the Darkness itself.

He has also amassed an encyclopaedic knowledge of every corner of Skylands that he has rescued – which, to be honest, is most of it by now.

Squidbeard

Captain Frightbeard's First Officer on-board the Phantom Tide.

Squiddlers

Googly-eyed pirate molluscs who fire exploding blowfish from their mortar guns. Ka-boom!

Squidface Brutes

Muscular, tentacle-faced pirates who carry enormous anchors on their backs just in case they have to poleaxe a landlubber or seven.

Stealth Elf

Stealth Elf's first memory is waking up in the hollow of a gnarled old tree. The young elf had no idea who she was or how she got there, so picked herself up, brushed herself down and started searching for answers. There were none to be found, although Stealth did stumble upon a mysterious elderly forest creature snoozing beside a lake. She tried to creep past, but didn't get far. As quick as a flash, the creature awoke, leapt from the ground and caught her

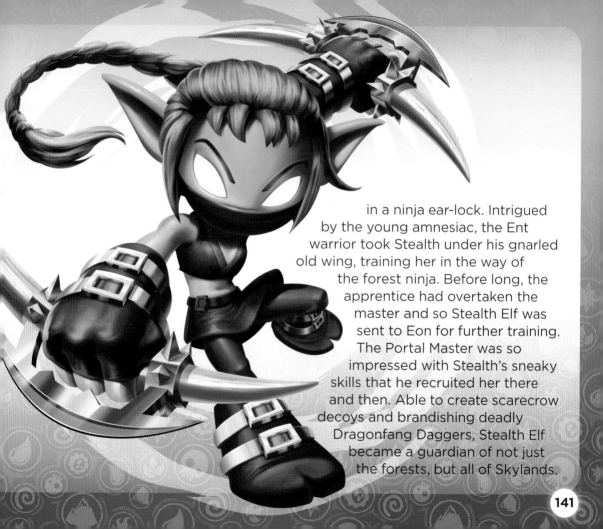

in a ninja ear-lock. Intrigued by the young amnesiac, the Ent warrior took Stealth under his gnarled old wing, training her in the way of the forest ninja. Before long, the apprentice had overtaken the master and so Stealth Elf was sent to Eon for further training. The Portal Master was so impressed with Stealth's sneaky skills that he recruited her there and then. Able to create scarecrow decoys and brandishing deadly Dragonfang Daggers, Stealth Elf became a guardian of not just the forests, but all of Skylands.

Storm Titans

The masters of the Cloud Kingdom. The Storm Titans are supposed to govern Skylands' weather systems, but instead spend most of their time playing games. Tut.

Stormy Stronghold

This Drow Fortress stood strong for generations until the evil elves tried to harness the power of the Eternal Air Source. The resulting tornado nearly ripped the place apart.

Story Scroll

Hidden all over Skylands, these yellowing scrolls of parchment reveal secrets of days gone by and hints of adventures yet to come.

Stump Smash

Going to sleep can be dangerous in Skylands. Take Stump Smash for example. One minute he was a happy, peaceful tree, taking a snooze in the warm summer sun. The next he had woken up to find that his entire forest had been chopped down by a team of lumberjack trolls. To make it worse, the loathsome loggers had removed all of his branches. All he had left was two massive mallets for hands. Anger rushing through his sap, Stump pulled his roots out of the ground and put his hammers to work, smashing the trolls' logging machines.

Once he was finished, he walloped the trolls too. He's still angry about what happened to him, but channels his anger into fighting evil with the Skylanders. Needless to say, trolls try their hardest to avoid this thumping tree.

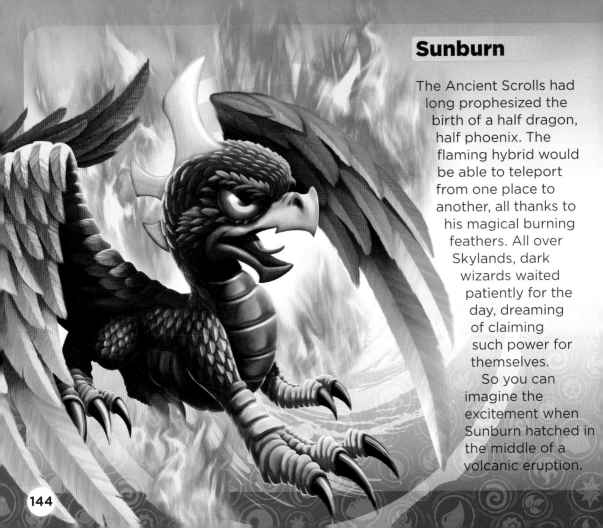

Sunburn

The Ancient Scrolls had long prophesized the birth of a half dragon, half phoenix. The flaming hybrid would be able to teleport from one place to another, all thanks to his magical burning feathers. All over Skylands, dark wizards waited patiently for the day, dreaming of claiming such power for themselves.

So you can imagine the excitement when Sunburn hatched in the middle of a volcanic eruption.

While the super-hot half-breed rested in his mother's nest, sorcerors, thieves and rascals were already climbing the volcano to snatch a handful of his potent plumage. Sunburn teleported to safety, but it wasn't long before they found him again. Even his flame-throwing abilities didn't put the bounders off. Eventually, Sunburn transported himself to Eon, who offered him both protection and a place in the Skylanders. Today, he regularly bakes baddies but also finds time to play practical jokes, teleporting behind his fellow Skylanders backs and playfully roasting their rumps.

against the Darkness, they were caught in the blast of the very volcano they were sworn to protect. Years later, when Kaos hatched the diabolical scheme to use the volcano to erupt Darkness throughout Skylands, the SWAP Force were called back into action – by you!

SWAP Force

Special Skylanders who defend the Cloudbreak Islands and have the ability to swap top and bottom halves with each other. The SWAP Force gained this power when, during an epic battle

Swarm

In a remote part of Skylands there is a humongous honeycomb pyramid, the home of a proud race of bee-like warriors. If you ever visit, you'll notice a big hole in its side. This was caused by Swarm, firstborn son of the hive's noble queen. As members of the royal family, neither Swarm nor any of his 9,000 brothers or sisters were allowed to leave the pyramid. Swarm, however, was unique. Unlike his waspish brethren, Swarm never stopped growing. Soon, the colony was too small for him and he burst through one of its honeycomb walls. Seeing the sky for the very first time, Swarm buzzed his wondrous wings and soared out into the air, never to return. Armed with a sting in his tail and able to blast barbed blades at bad guys, Swarm made a bee-line for the Skylanders and joined the Giants' fight against the Arkeyans.

Tt

T-Bone

A silly skeleton who thinks he's dead funny. Always cracking rib-ticklers, the only thing that wipes the smile off T-Bone's skull is scuttling spiders. The wicked web-heads are always stealing his bones.

Tech Element

Originally discovered by the Arkeyans, the Tech Element breathes life into machines. Tech Skylanders love tinkering with gadgets and gizmos.

Tech Spell Punks

Spell Punks who summon lasers from on high.

Terrabite

Terrafin's scrappy Sidekick.

Terrafin

This brawny boxer started out as a lifeguard on the shores of the Dirt Sea. But when an explosion transformed the sandy ocean into a sea of glass, a career change found Terrafin in the ring, where he won bout after bout of barmy boxing matches. While he was handy with his huge fists, Terrafin always got the drop on his opponents by burrowing beneath their feet and blasting up to deliver the final blow. Fighters came from miles around to challenge the champ, but Terrafin could never be defeated. Bored of bare-knuckle fighting, Terrafin threw in the towel to join the Skylanders and now only brawls with the forces of Darkness.

150

Thumpback

Although he was once a member of Captain Frightbeard's pirate crew, Thumpback never really liked pirating. He hated pillaging with a passion and wasn't even interested in buried treasure. The only perk to being a pirate was that he could regularly perch on the Phantom Tide's plank and fish. Using the ship's chain and anchor as a line and rod, Thumpback would sit there for hours, patiently waiting for the Leviathan Cloud Crab to take the bait. When it finally did, the colossal crustacean dragged Thumpback overboard and keelhauled him half way across Skylands. It was a lucky escape for Thumpback who avoided being trapped in the Chest of Exile with his ghastly shipmates. Instead, the barnacled Giant – who can spew up sea creatures at will – became one of the very first Skylanders.

Thumpling

Thumpback's Sidekick always has a whale of a time when fighting evil.

Time Twister Hourglass

One of the Skylanders' magic objects, this handy item slows down time.

Timidclopses

Cowardly cyclopses. These yellow-bellies will roll barrels at their enemies but will run and hide if they come face-to-face with a Skylander.

Tornados

Raging storms that whirl across the sky, destroying towns and even entire islands. However, the Mabu also use them as handy waste-disposal units, tossing their trash into passing twisters.

Toys

While trapped on Earth in their frozen state, Skylanders resemble harmless toys. Pop them on a Portal of Power and they'll zip back to Skylands to fight another day.

Tree of Life, the

A powerful tree with magical, life-giving properties. Its roots were the birthplace of Camo.

Tree Rex

Long before the Arkeyans came to power, Tree Rex was just another spectacular tree living in the ancient forests of Skylands. Then, as their power grew, the Arkeyans opened a factory in the nearby fields to produce their weapons of dark destruction. As the centuries rolled on, the Tech waste seeping from the weapons plant poisoned the forest. Tree Rex found himself mutating into a mighty Giant. His branches twisted into broad,

powerful arms and beams of pure sunlight burst from his eyes. Ripping himself away from his roots, Tree Rex raised the factory to the ground and stampeded over anyone who threatened the natural order of things. His green crusade made him an obvious choice to become one of the very first Skylanders.

Trees

Kaos believes that all trees are out to get him. And do you know what? They are!

153

Treetop Terrace

A vast forest bursting with life
– and the odd Drow witch too!

Trigger Happy

Trigger Happy by name, Trigger
Happy by nature. This giggling gremlin's
answer to everything is to shoot it
with gold coins from his gleaming
golden guns. Trigger Happy's cackling
laugh was first heard when a band of
dinosaur-riding bandits held up a bank
in a far-off frontier town. The outlaws

got more booty than they bargained for as Trigger Happy peppered them with gold bullion. The bandits ran screaming and the town-folk became instant millionaires as they gathered up Trigger Happy's shiny ammo. The giggling goldslinger swept across the plains, seeing off varmints and cleaning up crooks until a chance meeting with Eon saw him signed up as a Skylander.

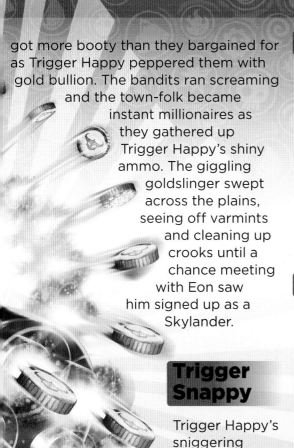

Trigger Snappy

Trigger Happy's sniggering Sidekick.

Trogmanders

Wizened green wizards who transform tiny Trog Pinchers into giant Trog Pinchers. Can also conjure up hordes of chomping Trogs when you least expect them.

Trog Pinchers

In their natural form, Trog Pinchers are pesky little critters with a nasty bite. But you don't want to face one after its been transmogrified by a Trogmander into a titanic toothy beast.

Trog Wanderers

Slow-moving shufflers who just fancy a bite . . . of you! Punch 'em and they'll shrink away to nothing.

Trolls

Trolls used to hide under bridges, making anyone who passed overhead pay a toll. However, as soon as the people of Skylands found out you could trick the troll-keepers by the use of a billy-goat, the bottom fell out of the bridge business. The trolls crawled out of the mud and started working for Kaos, building weapons and generally being bullies.

Troll Greasemonkeys

Maniacal troll mechanics who will bash you with their monkey wrenches as soon as look at you.

Troll Home Security

The troll security firm responsible for projecting a defensive force field around Kaos' Kastle. Went out of business when the Skylanders attacked.

Troll Stomper M5

This two-legged troll tank will stamp all over you if you get in its way. Then it'll blast you with rockets just in case you survived.

Troll Warehouse

A dank minefield-filled lair where the trolls stash all the junk that they steal.

Twin Water Spouts of Ocea Major-Minor, the

An essential component of the Core of Light, forged from the scales of the Leviathan itself.

Uu

Undead Element

The spookiest Element in all of Skylands, offering dominion over the powers of Undeath.

Ultrons

Arkeyan robot guards with laser-guided rocket launchers for hands.

Undead Spell Punks

Spell Punks who summon Rhu-Babies from a distant dimension, before turning them into Rhu-Barbs.

Unicorns

Beautiful steeds with magical horns erupting from their foreheads. Unicorn tails are often gathered by trolls for use in their diabolical weapons.

Upgrades

Fairy upgrades grant Skylanders new powers and abilities.

Vv

Vathek

The evil brother of the dragon king Ramses. Undead Vathek seized the Dragon Throne and turned his brother into stone. Defeated by Flavius and the Skylanders, he was transformed into a living statue himself.

Vindlevale

Winter never fell on Vindlevale until invading Ice Ogres built a giant wall of ice and blocked the sun.

Voodood

As a young Ooga Orc, Voodood entered the Cave of Trials to undergo the initiation rite of his tribe. Deep beneath the ground, he noticed a light pulsing in the distance. He followed the glow, descending deeper into the immense subterranean labyrinth, before stumbling into a huge, shining chamber. In the middle of the cavern, under a fierce magical spotlight, lay the skeleton of a dragon with a glittering gem where its heart should have been. Better still, the legendary Axe Reaver had been driven into the jewel. Voodood emerged from the Cave a hero, the dragon's skull fashioned into a stylish hat and the Axe Reaver in his hand. Taking his rightful place as chief, he led his people into battle against the Darkness. When the other Ooga were tragically wiped out, Eon gave shelter to the lone surviving warrior, welcoming him into the Skylanders.

Ww

Warnado

While still inside his egg, Warnado was plucked from his nest by a tornado and sent spinning into the sky. He hatched in the middle of the tempest but, instead of being tossed around the twister, he found himself able to control the storm. By the time he was back on solid ground, he had the ability to send himself into sensational spins, blasting enemies out of the way. In fact, if this turbulent turtle stays still for too long, he gets dizzy. How mixed up is that?

Water Element

The wettest of the magical Skylands Elements. Water Skylanders are usually happiest beneath the waves or skating around on freezing cold ice.

Water Spell Punks

Spell Punks who have mastered freezing drops of rain.

Weapon Master

Most believed that the imposing figure in the waters surrounding Eon's Citadel was just an Arkeyan statue, but when the Eternal Fire Source was restored the massive sculpture came back to life. The wise Weapon Master helped the Skylanders retrieve the last components of the Core of Light from their Arkeyan resting places.

Wendel

Following the disappearance of his father, Fargus, Wendel became the leader of the Mystic Seekers.

Wham-Shell

The crowned prince of the crustacean kingdom came to the throne at just the wrong time. The crab's underwater empire had been invaded by trolls who wanted to pump oil from the seabed. With his subjects scattered throughout the sea, Wham-Shell grabbed the claw-cracking Malacostracan Mace and declared war on all troll-kind. The trolls felt the sharp end of the mace while a barrage of exploding starfish destroyed their oilrigs. As the crabs started scuttling back to their home, Wham-Shell was responding to a greater calling – an offer from Eon to join the Skylanders.

Whirlwind

Half unicorn, half dragon, Whirlwind was spurned by both species. The unicorns turned their noses up at her feathery wings, while the dragons were envious of her splendid horn. So she soared into the sky, finding solace in passing storm clouds. Here, in the gusty gales, Whirlwind discovered she could harness extreme weather conditions. She could summon lightning-filled Tempest Clouds and blast rainbow energy from her enchanted horn.

Determined never to return home, Whirlwind was about to storm away when she heard cries from below. Trolls were swarming through the valley, lassoing unicorns and collecting dragon scales. Whirlwind swept in from above, unleashing a blinding rainbow that stunned the trolls into submission.

Both the dragons and unicorns welcomed Whirlwind home, but her gracious act also reached the ears of Eon. The Portal Master sent Lightning Rod to invite the dra-corn to become a Skylander. Today, trolls still get nervous when a storm brews in the skies.

Whisper Elf

Stealth Elf's ninja apprentice and Skylander sidekick.

Wilikins

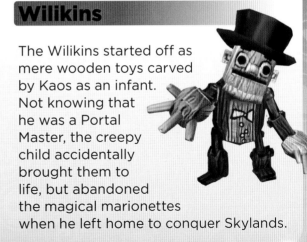

The Wilikins started off as mere wooden toys carved by Kaos as an infant. Not knowing that he was a Portal Master, the creepy child accidentally brought them to life, but abandoned the magical marionettes when he left home to conquer Skylands.

Wilikin Village

Scared his mother would discover that the Wilikins had come to life, Kaos built them a village on a nearby island. To keep his secret, Kaos also constructed a device that would return the wooden toys to their inanimate state whenever his dear old mum was near. Later, after her son had become supreme ruler of Skylands, Mother Kaos revealed she'd known about the Wilikins all along and employed many of them as servants. Wilikin Village was forgotten, and its inhabitants left in a deep slumber.

Windbag Djinnis

Mischievous clouds of dark magic that try to blow ships off course or zap passers-by with lightning strikes. Storm Titans use Windbags for target practice, considering them annoying pests.

Winged Boots

A magical item that gives a Skylander super-speed.

Winged Sapphires

Rare winged gems that are found fluttering throughout Skylands. Persephone is particularly fond of them, so gives the Skylanders discounts if they bring them to her.

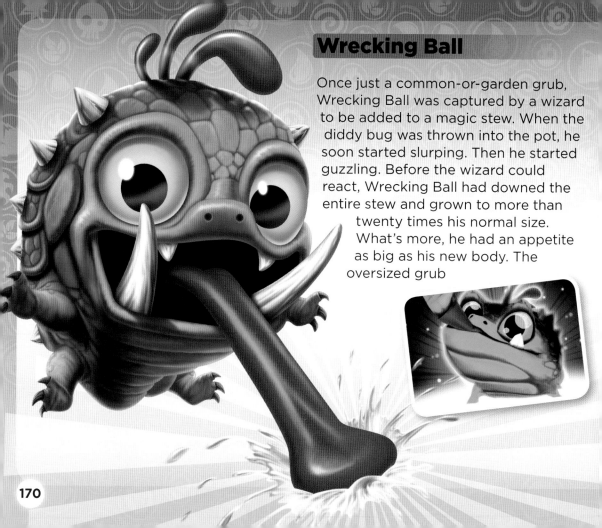

Wrecking Ball

Once just a common-or-garden grub, Wrecking Ball was captured by a wizard to be added to a magic stew. When the diddy bug was thrown into the pot, he soon started slurping. Then he started guzzling. Before the wizard could react, Wrecking Ball had downed the entire stew and grown to more than twenty times his normal size. What's more, he had an appetite as big as his new body. The oversized grub grabbed the sorcerer with his sticky tongue and swallowed the mage whole. Luckily for the wizard, Wrecking Ball didn't like the taste of beards, so spat him out again. Still famished, the reckless grub rolled into the Skylands countryside where he eventually ran into Eon. Actually, it's fairer to say he ran over Eon. Picking himself up, the Portal Master made Wrecking Ball a Skylander – but was careful to keep him away from the Citadel larder.

Xx

X Marks the Spot

The standard way of marking treasure on a pirate's map. For a while, buccaneers considered using a Q to mark the spot, but decided that it looked silly.

Yy

Zz

Yeti

Abominable snowmen come in many different varieties. There are two-armed Yeti, four-armed Yeti and, if you believe the rumours, 638-armed Yeti. Thank heavens they don't mind the cold. The gloves bill would be huge.

Zap

Born into a family of regal Water Dragons, Zap loved showing off in the waves. He came unstuck when a sudden riptide washed him out to sea, far away from his royal family. He drifted, scared and alone, until he was adopted by a shoal of electric eels. The freakish foster parents took him in and raised him as one of their own. They even helped him construct a shining gold harness that could hold an everlasting charge. As well as swimming faster than any sea-creature, Zap could now produce electrifying sea slime and pack a mean mega-volted punch. Even though the

cheeky champ was a shocking prankster, Eon soon recruited him as an amped-up Skylander.

Zook

While his Bambazooker brothers were happy just to stand around, Zook wanted to explore. Hoisting up his bamboo cannon, he squelched out of the mud and rushed into the forest. Before long, the Bambazookers started to hear stories about his exploits (particularly about the time he saved some elven explorers from a massive mountain troll). Thrilled by his heroics, the Bambazookers composed campfire songs about their wandering hero, but saved the best tunes for the news that Zook had become a Skylander.